Considering Adoption

A Biblical Perspective

A five-week small group study designed
to help couples explore God's perspective on
making an adoption decision.

Doug and Amy Martin and Jason and Trisha Weber

Table of Contents

Considering Adoption

Printed in the United States of America.
ISBN: 1-572-29724-7
ISBN-13: 978-157229-724-1
16 15 14 13 12 11 10 09 08 07 06 2 3 4 5 6 7

FamilyLife

5800 Ranch Drive
Little Rock, AR 72223
1-800-FL-TODAY
www.familylife.com

About the Authors

Doug and Amy Martin are the parents of six children, two of which were adopted through the state foster care system. They live in Brentwood, Tenn., where Doug serves as community group pastor for Fellowship Bible Church. Doug and Amy previously served FamilyLife for eight years, where they helped found FamilyLife's Hope for Orphans ministry.

Jason and Trisha Weber are graduates in social work from the University of Kansas. They served in the inner city ministry of Campus Crusade for Christ for seven years and worked with many families and children involved in the foster care system. They became foster parents and adopted twin daughters who now reside with them in Little Rock, Ark., where they work with FamilyLife's Hope for Orphans.

Acknowledgments

Doug and Amy Martin

A HUGE thank you to Dave Boehi: Bo, thanks for sharing your gift of the written word. Your editing skills are second to none.

To Abby, Meredith, Dan, Micheal, Hope and Alex: You are a blessing! What a joy it is to be your parents and to walk through the miracle of adoption together! You are awesome children!!

To Matt and Tammy Winkler: Thank you for modeling Christ in your own journey of adoption. We have watched you closely and have learned much. You have been an ongoing source of blessing, encouragement, and sanity for our family. We love you, Winklers!

To Paul and Robin Pennington: We are so thankful our lives and families intersected just three years ago. You two are the most humble, obedient and knowledgeable "experts" we know on adoption. God has used you to impact literally thousands of children and families for the Kingdom ... including our own. Thanks for walking the talk.

And to our Heavenly Father: Thank you for not leaving us as orphans when you chose to adopt us into your family ... for choosing us, not because we were loveable or worthy, but because we were not.

Jason and Trisha Weber

To Dave Boehi: Dave, you are wonderful to work with. God has used your incredible gifts time and time again to make an eternal difference in the lives of others.

To the Penningtons and the Martins: Thank you for your courage and your vision in starting Hope for Orphans and for your continual encouragement of us. We are grateful that you have allowed us to be a part of what God is doing.

To the staff team of Here's Life Inner City: Thank you for teaching us about God's heart for "the least of these" and for living it out every day.

To our Heavenly Father who adopted us despite all of our special needs and who gave us two of the greatest treasures we could have ever imagined in our little girls: Thank you.

To children everywhere who wait another night without a forever family: We pray that you would know God, your heavenly Father. He sees you, He knows you, He loves you.

Before You Begin

Thank you for deciding to invest your time in exploring the miracle of adoption! Participating in this small group will help you and your spouse work through the many issues involved in coming to a biblically informed adoption decision. We trust that the others in your group will provide a much needed network of support as you think and pray through God's will for your life concerning adoption.

You could complete this study with your spouse, but we strongly urge you to either form or join a group of couples studying this material. You will find that the questions in each session help create a special environment of encouragement as you seek together to follow God's will for your lives.

There are only four ground rules for HomeBuilders group members:

- Share nothing that will embarrass your spouse.
- You may pass on any question.
- Anything shared in the group stays in the group.
- Complete the HomeBuilders Project with your spouse between each session.

May God bless you on your new journey!

Notes To Group Leaders

1. Additional copies of *Exploring Adoption* are available for purchase from FamilyLife at $4.99 each.
To place an order, refer to the information on page two.

2. Leading a group is much easier than you may think! A group leader in a HomeBuilders session is really just a facilitator. As a leader, your goal is simply to guide the group through the discussion questions. You don't need to teach the material—in fact, we don't want you to! The special dynamic of a HomeBuilders group is that couples teach themselves.

3. Be sure to read the Leader's Tips in Appendix B for additional information on:
   - Leading a session
   - Inviting others to participate in a study
   - Handling child care
   - Leading a study in your church
   - Answering the most commonly asked questions about leading a group

4. Before each session, refer to the Leader's Notes in Appendix C for comments on specific questions in each session.

5. To create an atmosphere that is friendly and comfortable, it is recommended that you do this study in a home setting. In many cases the couple that is leading the study also serves as host to the group. Sometimes involving another couple as host is a good idea. Choose whatever option you feel will work best for your group, taking into account factors such as the number of couples participating and the location.

6. The material presented in each session is designed for a 90-minute study; however, we recommend a two-hour block of time. This will allow you to have time for fellowship and refreshments and still move through each part of the study at a more relaxed pace.

7. It is important to start and end your sessions on time. Also, it is important for couples to commit to attending all five sessions and to completing each of the HomeBuilders projects.

8. An excellent resource that provides greater detail on leading a HomeBuilders group is the *HomeBuilders Leader's Guide* by Drew and Kit Coons. This book may be purchased through FamilyLife.

A Note from the Authors

Their names are Micheal and Alex Martin and Carmen and Cecilia Weber. These are the children that God in His infinite wisdom and goodness placed in our families through the miracle of adoption.

For both of our families, however, our adoption journey didn't end with the adoption of these children. In many ways, it was just the beginning. The experience of adoption served to open our eyes more and more to God's heart. It also served to open our eyes to the overwhelming need in our world for those of us who follow Christ to consider what God might have us do in the life of a child who needs a forever family. We have met numerous Christian couples who have at one time or another considered adoption. However, something happened to stop many of these couples short in their adoption pursuit. What was it?

Adoption can feel like an overwhelming process and Christians often stop because they are never able to have their questions, fears and uncertainties addressed adequately from a biblical perspective. We have written this study with the hope that your group's discussion will remove some of those obstacles as you seek God's will in this area.

This will not be a "how to" manual for the adoption process. Rather it will provide an opportunity for you and your spouse to interact in an encouraging and safe environment about the adoption issues that are closest to both your heart and God's. Our prayer for you is that this study will help you make a God directed decision about whether adopting a child is part of God's plan for your life. And if it is not, we trust that this study will, at the very least, help you to know a little more of God's heart.

Starting the Adoption Dialogue

W A R M • U P   15   M I N U T E S

1. Go around the room and introduce yourselves, starting with the person with the most recent speeding ticket. Also, answer the following question:

If you were a car, what type of car would you like to be? Be specific.

2. In keeping with the car analogy, as you begin this group study on adoption, choose which of the following best characterizes where you are in the "adoption process":

Reverse: Not interested

Park: Not against it, but no plans to go anywhere right now.

Neutral: No strong feeling one way or the other. Just fact finding right now.

Drive: Some interest. Moving forward. Have taken some initial exploratory steps.

Overdrive: We are definitely adopting. Get in, sit down, and hold on!

Attitudes About Adoption

1. When someone mentions the word "adoption," what are the first words or phrases that come to mind?

2. Were you adopted? If so what was it like for you growing up as an adopted child?

3. Do you know anyone who has adopted? From your perspective, what are the positive and negative aspects of adoption?

4. How does your perspective of adoption compare with your spouse's attitude?

The "Dragger" and the "Draggee"

One of the greatest values in participating in a group like this is the opportunity to talk with your spouse and with other couples about adoption. Having lots of questions about adoption is normal. Questions may be different or similar, but we all have them. Some are more practical, "how to" questions, and others are more relational and emotional.

As a general rule, when a couple is considering adoption, one of you has more questions and more hesitation, while the other is eager and motivated. We call this the "dragger" and "draggee" scenario—one person is dragging the other!

Case Study

On a weekday evening, James and Emily arrive at an adoption workshop at their church.

Emily: I'm so excited about this workshop! You know, I just really believe God may want us to adopt a child. Everywhere I turn I'm running into another family with adopted kids. It's made me seriously wonder if we should consider adoption as well.

James: So ... how long is this meeting scheduled to last?

Emily: Just 90 minutes.

James: But...the game starts in an hour!

Emily: Here, take one of these pre-adoption application forms. While we're waiting for the workshop to start, I thought we could fill them out.

James: Applications? Don't you think it's a bit premature to be filling out applications? I mean, we really haven't even talked about it. I'm not sure I'm ready for another mouth to feed. Besides, do you know how much adoptions cost?

Emily: We're not committing to anything … yet. It's just this feeling I have. Think about it: Our new child might be waiting for us right now in some foster home across town or in orphanage in Guatemala. Isn't that mind-boggling?

James: Our child is in Guatemala? We never talked about getting a child from overseas. In fact, we haven't really talked about this at all. Besides, have you checked our finances lately? We don't exactly have extra cash laying around anywhere … unless, of course, you've also opened some secret adoption account in Switzerland …

Emily: Here, my portion of the application is done. Want me to help you fill in your part? What's your social security number?

Instructor: Welcome to the Exploring Adoption workshop … tonight is going to be an informative couple of hours …

James: (Whispering) A couple of hours? So much for the game.

Emily: Stop whining! You can watch games on television any other night of the week. Here, put these applications away for now. We'll finish them later.

James: Yeah, much later …

5. Which character in the above scenario do you most identify with Emily (the dragger) or James (the draggee)? Why?

6. What do think about the dragger's approach? If you were the dragger in the scenario, how would your approach be similar or different?

7. What do you think of the draggee's response? If you were the draggee in the scenario, how might you respond?

8. If the couple in this Case Study went ahead and adopted a child and nothing changed in their attitudes, what problems would they face?

"Pure and undefiled religion"

9. Read James 1:27 and Psalm 10:14. What do these verses communicate about how God considers adoption?

Pure and lasting religion in the sight of God our Father means that we must care for orphans and widows in their troubles, and refuse to let the world corrupt us.
> —James 1:27 (NLT)

But you, O God, do see trouble and grief; you consider it to take it in hand. The victim commits himself to you; you are the helper of the fatherless.
> —Psalm 10:14 (NIV)

10. Why do you think God calls caring for the orphan pure and lasting religion?

11. Now read Ephesians 1:3-6 and Romans 8:15-16:

Blessed be the God and Father of our Lord Jesus Christ, who has blessed us with every spiritual blessing in the heavenly places in Christ, just as He chose us in Him before the foundation of the world, that we would be holy and blameless before Him. In love He predestined us to adoption as sons through Jesus Christ to Himself, according to the kind intention of His will, to the praise of the glory of His grace, which He freely bestowed on us in the Beloved.
          —Ephesians 1:3-6

For you have not received a spirit of slavery leading to fear again, but you have received a spirit of adoption as sons by which we cry out, "Abba! Father!" The Spirit Himself testifies with our spirit that we are children of God.
          —Romans 8:15-16

What do these passages tell us about the subject of adoption?

12. Earlier in this session you were asked, "Were you adopted?" How would you answer that question now?

Throughout the Bible, God instructs us to care for the orphan—He calls it pure and lasting religion. Adoption is one way to care for orphans which God Himself modeled when He adopted us as His sons and daughters.

Take a moment and write:

- What intrigues or excites you the most about considering adoption.
- What causes you the most fear, uncertainty, or doubt.

Be honest. After writing your answers, huddle with your spouse and share your thoughts with each other.

Make a Date

Make a date with your spouse to meet before the next session to complete the HomeBuilders Project. Your leader will ask you to share something from this experience.

_____

DATE

_____

TIME

_____

LOCATION

HOMEBUILDERS PROJECT   6 o   M I N U T E S

Individually:

1. Look at the Case Study in the Blueprints section. As you and your spouse consider adoption, is there a "dragger" and a "draggee" in your relationship? Which are you? What issues or questions are you dealing with right now as you look at this issue?

2. What can you do to meet the needs of your spouse? What can your spouse do to meet your needs?

Interact as a couple:

1. Share your answers from the previous section.

2. Share any new insights gained from the first Blueprints session.

The Heart of God

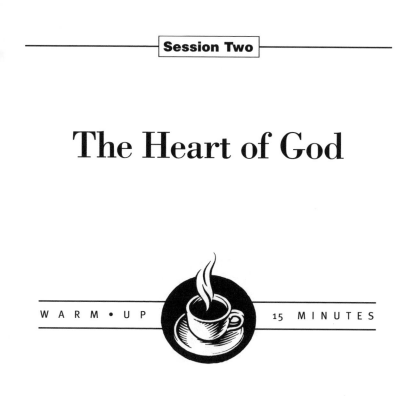

WARM · UP   15 MINUTES

1. What was one of the primary things your spouse did during dating or courtship that won your heart?

2. What is your favorite season of the year and why?

3. If you could do anything with a good friend (other than your spouse) for a week, what would it be?

4. What one thing (besides God) would you say you are most passionate about in life?

5. Share one thing you learned from the last session's HomeBuilders Project.

BLUEPRINTS   6o MINUTES

Priority List

Getting to know someone's likes, dislikes, and passions helps us know a little more of that person's heart. In the same way, getting to know God's likes, dislikes, and passions helps us to know His heart.

Consider the following quote from C. Thomas Davis in his book, *Fields of the Fatherless*:
> *"If you searched the Bible from front to back, you'd find many issues close to God's heart. But you'd also notice three groups of people coming up again and again.*

They appear so many times, in fact, you have to conclude that God mentions them purposely to make sure they are at the top of our priority list."

Let's take a closer look at these three groups of people.

1. Read the following passages from Scripture:

You shall not wrong a stranger or oppress him, for you were strangers in the land of Egypt. You shall not afflict any widow or orphan.
—Exodus 22:21-22

For the LORD your God is the God of gods and the Lord of lords, the great, the mighty, and the awesome God who does not show partiality nor take a bribe. He executes justice for the orphan and the widow, and shows His love for the alien by giving him food and clothing.
—Deuteronomy 10:17-18

Thus says the LORD, "Do justice and righteousness, and deliver the one who has been robbed from the power of his oppressor. Also do not mistreat or do violence to the stranger, the orphan, or the widow; and do not shed innocent blood in this place."
—Jeremiah 22:3

Why do you think God has such a strong concern for widows, orphans, and strangers? What do these three groups have in common?

2. Many of us do not know how it feels to be an orphan or widow. But anyone can relate to the experience of being a stranger or outsider. Choose one of the following scenarios that you may have experienced:

- Attending a new school
- Starting a new job
- Driving in an unfamiliar town and trying to find a particular location...after dark
- Visiting a country where you do not speak the language and you don't know how to get anywhere.

How do you feel in these types of situations? If you can, tell the group about an experience of feeling like a stranger or outsider.

3. What helped you make adjustments so you no longer felt like a stranger?

God's Help

4. One of the words you may have used to describe how you felt in one of the above scenarios is "helpless." Deuteronomy 24:19-22 describes God's provision of help for these groups:

> *"When you reap your harvest in your field and have forgotten a sheaf in the field, you shall not go back to get it; it shall be for the alien, for the orphan, and for the widow, in order that the LORD your God may bless you in all the work of your hands. When you beat your olive tree, you shall not go over the boughs again; it shall be for the alien, for the orphan, and for the widow. When you gather the grapes of your vineyard, you shall not go over it again; it shall be for the alien, for the orphan, and for the widow. You shall remember that you were a slave in the land of Egypt; therefore I am commanding you to do this thing."*

Since God gives us the responsibility to ensure these groups of people are provided for, what are some creative ways that we can leave the sheaves in the field, the olives in the branches, and the grapes on the vine in order to help provide for the needs of these groups?

5. How does Proverbs 23:10-11 describe God as it relates to the orphan?

Do not move the ancient boundary or go into the fields of the fatherless, for their Redeemer is strong; He will plead their case against you.

6. We see examples of "defense" in everything from sports to the court room. What are some words that you generally associate with the word "defend?"

7. Why does a child without a family need "defending"? What are some of the things that can happen to children without parents?

HomeBuilders Principle:
God reserves a special place in His heart for orphans and calls us to help defend and protect them.

Our Adoption

As we saw in the last session, the Bible uses the metaphor of adoption to describe what God has done for us through Christ. Ephesians 1:5 tells us, "He predestined us to adoption as sons through Jesus Christ to Himself, according to the kind intention of His will . . ."

8. What do you think it means that we have been adopted as sons through Jesus Christ?

Why do you think a word like "adoption" is used to describe what happens to us when we come to know Christ?

9. If you know Christ as your Savior and Lord, tell the group what your life was like before God worked in your heart to draw you to Him. In what ways was your life similar to that of an orphan?

Read the following passages:

The fool has said in his heart, "There is no God." They are corrupt, they have committed abominable deeds; there is no one who does good. The LORD has looked down from heaven upon the sons of men to see if there are any who understand, who seek after God. They have all turned aside, together they have become corrupt; there is no one who does good, not even one.
—Psalm 14:1-3

But God demonstrates His own love toward us, in that while we were yet sinners, Christ died for us.
—Romans 5:8

1. What criteria did you meet in order for God to be willing to adopt you?

2. What criteria do people often list as they consider who they would adopt?

3. What would have happened if God had used some of these criteria in His decision to adopt us?

HomeBuilders Principle:
God adopts us not because we were the cutest, the smartest, or were at the least risk of failure. Rather, He adopted us despite our dysfunction and failures and undesirable characteristics.

Make a Date

Make a date with your spouse to meet before the next session to complete the HomeBuilders Project. Your leader will ask you to share from this experience.

_____
DATE

_____
TIME

_____
LOCATION

HOMEBUILDERS PROJECT   6 0   M I N U T E S

Individually:

1. Have you thought much before this study about our responsibility as believers to care for orphans, widows, and strangers? Why or why not?

2. In what way does learning about God's heart affect your view of adoption?

As a Couple:

1. Share your answers from the individual section.

2. Look again at the Wrap-Up section of the group session. What are some criteria you have placed on children who you might be willing to adopt? List 3-5 characteristics.

3. If you applied the same standard to fatherless children that God applied to you, how would that change the kind of child you bring into your family?

4. Spend a few minutes in prayer as a couple, asking God to lead in your family regarding any decisions you are making about adoption.

Addressing Concerns About Adoption

W A R M • U P   15   M I N U T E S

Blindfold one person and lead him (or her) to another room. Hide an object such as a candy bar in the room where you are meeting, and designate one person as the "guide." Bring the blindfolded person back into the room, and tell him his goal is to find the candy bar based on the instructions from the group. One person (the guide) will provide correct directions, while everyone else simultaneously shouts out incorrect directions. However, do not do not tell blindfolded person which person is the guide.

After completing the exercise ask the following questions:

1. How did you feel when everyone was yelling different instructions at you?

2. We live in a culture with many voices and opinions. Regarding adoption, what are some of the questions and objections people raise to those considering adopting a child?

3. Share one thing that you learned from last session's HomeBuilders Project.

BLUEPRINTS   60 MINUTES

Outside Advice

There are many different opinions about adoption and adopted children within our culture. You may have heard many of these "voices" coming from the media, your community, your friends, and your family. It is important to recognize that these voices exist and determine which ones you should be listening to.

1. Which of the issues mentioned in the Warm Up section have you struggled with?

2. What kinds of advice are you getting from friends and family concerning adoption?

3. What general concerns do you have about bringing an adopted child into your family?

4. What financial concerns do you have concerning adoption?

5. How much are these concerns affecting the process of making your decision about adoption?

Some of the concerns associated with adoption are founded on reliable information. However, there are many other issues that surface as a result of myths that have crept into the adoption landscape. These "myth" issues can often be addressed by simply gathering better information.

For example, one myth is that a couple must have considerable financial resources in order to adopt. However, adoption grant programs, employer adoption benefits, the federal income tax credit, and reductions or removal of fees for children with special needs and children in the foster care system can make adoption affordable for almost anyone willing to pursue the available options.

For more information regarding myths about adoption, visit www.familylife.com (click on the Hope for Orphans quicklink). Read our adoption guide entitled "Welcome Home: Eight Steps to Adoption."

Whether the concerns that are being raised are legitimate or are based largely on myth, it is important to learn to discern what voices to listen to.

Trusting in God Through the Adoption Process

6. Read through the following Scripture passages, and for each one answer the following question: How does this passage help address some of the concerns we have about adoption?

Be anxious for nothing, but in everything by prayer and supplication with thanksgiving let your requests be made known to God. And the peace of God, which surpasses all comprehension, will guard your hearts and your minds in Christ Jesus. Finally, brethren, whatever is true, whatever is honorable, whatever is right, whatever is pure, whatever is lovely, whatever is of good repute, if there is any excellence and if anything worthy of praise, dwell on these things.
—Philippians 4:6-8

I can do all things through Him who strengthens me.
—Philippians 4:13

Consider it all joy, my brethren, when you encounter various trials, knowing that the testing of your faith produces endurance. And let endurance have its perfect result, so that you may be perfect and complete, lacking in nothing. But if any of you lacks wisdom, let him ask of God, who gives to all generously and without reproach, and it will be given to him. But he must ask in faith without any doubting, for the one who doubts is like the surf of the sea, driven and tossed by the wind. For that man ought not to expect that he will receive anything from the Lord,
— James 1:2-7

"Do not worry then, saying, 'What will we eat?' or 'What will we drink?' or 'What will we wear for clothing?' For the Gentiles eagerly seek all these things; for your heavenly Father knows that you need all these things. But seek first His kingdom and His righteousness, and all these things will be added to you. So do not worry about tomorrow; for tomorrow will care for itself. Each day has enough trouble of its own.
　　　　　　　　　　　　—Matthew 6:31-34

Now faith is the assurance of things hoped for, the conviction of things not seen. For by it the men of old gained approval. By faith we understand that the worlds were prepared by the word of God, so that what is seen was not made out of things which are visible.
　　　　　　　　　　　　—Hebrews 11:1-3

7. It is also very common for potential adoptive parents to wonder whether they have the ability to adopt a child with additional needs. We ask ourselves questions like, "Do I have what it takes?" or, "Will I be able to love an adopted child the same?" or, "How will I know what to do?"

Read Exodus 4:10-17. How does this passage relate to such questions?

*Then Moses said to the LORD, "Please, Lord, I
have never been eloquent, neither recently nor in
time past, nor since You have spoken to Your
servant; for I am slow of speech and slow of
tongue." The LORD said to him, "Who has made
man's mouth? Or who makes him mute or deaf,
or seeing or blind? Is it not I, the LORD? "Now
then go, and I, even I, will be with your mouth,
and teach you what you are to say." But he said,
"Please, Lord, now send the message by whomever
You will." Then the anger of the LORD burned
against Moses, and He said, "Is there not your
brother Aaron the Levite? I know that he speaks
fluently. And moreover, behold, he is coming out to
meet you; when he sees you, he will be glad in his
heart. You are to speak to him and put the words
in his mouth; and I, even I, will be with your
mouth and his mouth, and I will teach you what
you are to do. Moreover, he shall speak for you to
the people; and he will be as a mouth for you and
you will be as God to him. You shall take in your
hand this staff, with which you shall perform the
signs."*

—Exodus 4:10-17

Of all the Scriptures that we have discussed, which one
do you think is most helpful to apply to your own
circumstances?

Dealing With Objections

Case Study

Don and Angela had two biological girls aged 7 and 11 when they began to sense that God was leading them to adopt a 5-year old boy from Russia. They had been praying for some time and had been including their daughters in the discussion. Everyone was excited and looked forward to announcing the news to the grandparents. But when the family told Angela's parents over dinner one night, the conversation grew coldly silent. The girls continued to talk about how much they were looking forward to a little brother but Angela's parents hardly said a word.

Later that night after the girls went to bed, Angela's father became very upset. "How could you possibly take such a beautiful family and ruin it by bringing in someone else's kid? This child will bring every problem he has had in his life into your home! He is not your problem. You have a responsibility before God to provide for and protect your little girls. You are making a huge mistake."

Angela's mother added, "You all barely fit in your house as it is. How are you going to add another body and another mouth to feed? Adoption is expensive anyway—you are going to go broke paying for it."

8. What do you think is motivating Angela's parents to respond this way?

9. What is the best way for Don and Angela to handle the situation?

10. As you consider the possibility of adoption, how are you handling (or planning to handle) objections from your family and friends?

Repeat the scenario of the Warm Up. Blindfold the
same person and hide the candy bar in a different
place. This time, tell the blindfolded person what voice
is giving him the proper instructions; you might even
have that person say a few words at the beginning. Ask
the group to yell wrong directions again. After the
blindfolded person has found the candy bar, ask the
following questions:

1. What was different when you knew who to listen to?

2. When it comes to making an adoption decision who
should we ultimately be listening to?

In our next session, we'll talk more about listening to
God during this process.

Make a Date

Make a date with your spouse to meet before the next session to complete the HomeBuilders Project. Your leader will ask you to share from this experience.

_____
DATE

_____
TIME

_____
LOCATION

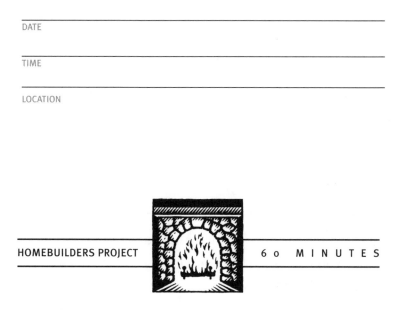

HOMEBUILDERS PROJECT　　　　　6 0　 M I N U T E S

Individually:

1. On a sheet of paper, list the different concerns you have as you consider adoption.

2. How has the response of friends and family affected your thought process?

3. Look again at the Scripture passages we discussed in questions 6-7 of the Blueprints section. Which passages left the biggest impression with you?

As a couple:

1. Share your answers from the individual section.

2. Psalm 105:5 says that it is important to remember all that God has done for us. Make a list together of the things you have seen God provide for in the past and different difficult circumstances that you have seen God bring you through. Spend some time praying together and thanking Him for how He has provided for you.

Making a Decision About Adoption

WARM • UP   15   MINUTES

1. Choose one of the following questions to answer:

What was one of the most difficult decisions you have ever made (either as a couple or individually)? Why was the decision so difficult?

What would you say was one of the most important decisions you've ever made about the direction of your life?

2. Looking back, what has been the impact of the decision on your life?

3. Share one thing that you learned from the HomeBuilders Project from last session.

The importance of being like-minded in your decision making

1. What gets you most excited about the possibility of adoption? What gives you the most anxiety?

2. Read Philippians 2:1-2:

> *Therefore if there is any encouragement in Christ, if there is any consolation of love, if there is any fellowship of the Spirit, if any affection and compassion, make my joy complete by being of the same mind, maintaining the same love, united in spirit, intent on one purpose.*

Why do you think it's important to be like-minded with your spouse as you consider adoption or orphan care?

3. What would be the long-term implications of moving forward with a decision to adopt even if you are not like-minded?

The Importance of Seeking Direction from God

> Psalm 31:3 *tells us, "For You are my rock and my fortress; for Your name's sake You will lead me and guide me."* And Psalm 32:8 says, *"I will instruct you and teach you in the way which you should go; I will counsel you with My eye upon you."* Throughout the Scriptures it is clear that God will provide direction and guidance as we walk through life. Usually this guidance comes from His Word, but other occasions it may come from the inner leading of the Holy Spirit. James 1:5 says, *"But if any of you lacks wisdom, let him ask of God, who gives to all generously and without reproach, and it will be given to him."*

We need to ask God for wisdom. In other words we need to pray. And as you do, here are a few steps you can take to seek direction from Him.

Step One: Gather information.

4. Proverbs 13:16 tells us, *"Every prudent man acts out of knowledge" (NIV).* As you consider adding to your family through adoption, what information do you need to make an informed decision?

Step Two: Seek counsel.

5. Read Proverbs 11:14:

"Where there is no guidance the people fall, but in abundance of counselors there is victory."

How would you apply this passage to your present situation? How has participating in this group helped you?

6. One of the best resources to help you understand adoption is talking with couples who have already adopted. Is there a couple you know and trust who you could approach about walking with you through the adoption journey? If not, how could you find a couple?

Step Three: *Evaluate desires and circumstances.*

Philippians 2:13 reads, *"for it is God who is at work in you, both to will and to work for His good pleasure."* It could be that God has given you a desire to adopt, and you need to listen to that desire no matter what fears you may have. At the same time, evaluating your present circumstances may help you discern whether this is a wise decision.

Answer the following questions individually, and then share your answers with your spouse:

7. Up to this point, what would you say has been your desire about adoption?

8. As you look at the circumstances of your present situation in life, would you say they would support a decision to adopt? Explain.

***Step Four: Ask yourself if you are willing to
follow God's direction.***

Some Christians stumble at this point when asking God
for direction. You see it in the man who says, "I'm
willing to obey you, God, as long as it doesn't mean
confessing my mistakes to my wife," or in the parents
who pray, "God, use my child to reach others for Christ
... but I don't want him to move to Africa."

George Mueller, a noted Christian leader in the 19th
century, once wrote that, when he is seeking God's will,

> *I seek at the beginning to get my heart into such a
> state that it has no will of its own in regard to a
> given matter. Nine-tenths of the trouble with
> people generally is just here. Nine-tenths of the
> difficulties are overcome when our hearts are
> ready to do the Lord's will, whatever it may be.
> When one is truly in this state, it is usually but a
> little way to the knowledge of what His will is.*

***Step Five: As you prayerfully work through all
these steps, ask God to guide you through the
person of the Holy Spirit.***

9. What do the following passages tell us about the role of the Holy Spirit in our lives?

> *"But when He, the Spirit of truth, comes, He will guide you into all the truth; for He will not speak on His own initiative, but whatever He hears, He will speak; and He will disclose to you what is to come."*
>
> —John 16:13

> *"But the Helper, the Holy Spirit, whom the Father will send in My name, He will teach you all things, and bring to your remembrance all that I said to you."*
>
> —John 14:26

God often speaks through Scripture, and on some occasions He speaks to our hearts through the Spirit, giving us a conviction of His will.

If you can, share about a time in your life when you discerned God's direction regarding important decision making.

Note: It is important to recognize that God uses these different steps together to reveal His will. It's best not to single out one step as exclusively revealing God's plan. Also, it is easy for some people to mistake selfish desires for the "voice of the Spirit." The Spirit's internal guidance must always be consistent with His character and ministry. That means three things will always be true of His leading:

- It will glorify Christ.
- It will promote holiness.
- It will be consistent with God's Word.

HomeBuilders Principle:
When making a decision about adoption, it is necessary to discern God's direction.

Is the issue really obedience?

10. Read the following passages:

"Vindicate the weak and fatherless; Do justice to the afflicted and destitute."
—Psalm 82:3 (NIV)

"Religion that God our father accepts as pure and faultless is this: to look after orphans and widows in their distress and to keep oneself from being polluted by the world."

—James 1:27(NIV)

After reading these verses, do you see the decision to "look after orphans" as an issue of obedience or a personal preference? Why?

11. How does this understanding affect your decision about adoption?

12. It's important to note that adoption is not the only obedient response to these passages. What are some specific ways believers can fulfill James 1:27, God's instruction to look after the orphan?

Here are a few final suggestions on making the
adoption decision:

- Engage in open, honest dialogue with your
  spouse concerning adoption. Are there any
  unresolved questions, fears or concerns?

*"Search me, O God, and know my heart; test me
and know my anxious thoughts. See if there is
any offensive way in me, and lead me in the way
everlasting."*
—Psalm 139:23-24 (NIV)

- Commit your decision to prayer, both
  individually and as a couple.

*Trust in the Lord with all your heart and lean not
on your own understanding. In all your ways
acknowledge Him, and He will make your paths
straight.*
—Proverbs 3:5-6 (NIV)

- Do not make a decision to move forward unless you are like-minded.

- Be willing to be obedient ... even if it means saying "no" to adoption. Remember adoption is not for everyone.

- If God is not calling you to adopt, talk about how you can be involved in orphan care as God has instructed all believers.

Make a Date

Make a date with your spouse to meet before the next session to complete the HomeBuilders Project. Your leader will ask you to share something from this experience.

DATE

TIME

LOCATION

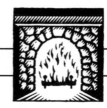
Obedience to God's will is the secret of spiritual knowledge and insight. It is not willingness to know, but willingness to DO God's will that brings certainty.

—Eric Liddell, missionary

Individually:

1. Look back over the material we discussed in the Blueprints section. If you were going to make an adoption decision today, what would it be, and why?

2. What additional information do you need to make an informed adoption decision?

3. What would you say are your primary obstacles to adopting a child?

4. If you were to decide not to adopt, what is another practical way you, as a couple, can care for the orphans?

As a couple:

1. Share your answers from the individual section.

2. End your time together praying for God's direction and for courage to be obedient.

Where Do We Go From Here?

W A R M • U P   4 5   M I N U T E S

As we discussed in Session Four, making a decision about adoption can be a complicated and difficult journey. It is possible and even probable that the last four sessions have left you with more questions than you had at the beginning. The hope is that now, however, you are equipped with the right questions to make an informed and God-honoring adoption decision.

1. How has God spoken to you over the last several weeks concerning His will in the area of adoption?

2. Has there been anything during these weeks together that has transformed your thinking about God, the orphan, or adoption?

3. What are two or three main obstacles or questions that you are going to have to address as you continue your adoption journey?

After each couple discusses their answers to these questions, have someone pray for this couple.

To Adoption and Beyond

Whether you sense God is calling you to adopt or not, you may be wondering about other ways to be obedient in caring for the "least of these" and specifically the orphan.

Across the country people like you are seeing God do astonishing things through their small steps of obedience on behalf of the orphan. Consider the following real life case study:

Jay and Suzanne were adoptive parents in a small Texas town church who sensed that God wanted them to go beyond the adoption of children into their own family and make a difference for the orphan in even bigger ways.

At first Suzanne used a church bulletin board to display information and pictures of waiting children to make the congregation aware of the needs of orphans.

Soon she started a Christian support group for families with adopted children in the community, and the new ministry grew so rapidly that they outgrew their facility.

Even though the support group was going well, God's work had only just begun. Suzanne's greatest desire was to see children adopted. She went to the elder board of her church to propose a hosting program in which children from an orphanage in Kazakhstan would be brought to the United States to live with families for a month. This would give each child the opportunity to experience being a part of a family, and the family an opportunity to consider adopting that child.

Some in the church gave money, some gave clothes, and some hosted children. Regardless of their role, members made the necessary sacrifices to bring 29 children from Kazakhstan for a visit, with the intention of finding them permanent homes. In the end, some couples decided to adopt more, and altogether more than 40 Kazakh children found homes in Texas.

This ministry has already grown far beyond Suzanne's expectations. "If more than forty children could get families in a small Texas town where people wear cowboy boots and drive pickup trucks," says Suzanne, "think about what other churches could do."

*Adapted from "His Heart, Our Hands," Familylife's guide to establishing and growing orphans ministry in the local church.

1. As Jay and Suzanne watched God orchestrate the remarkable circumstances that brought more than 40 orphans to forever families in their little church, how would you think their personal faith was affected?

2. In what ways do you think this journey and these children have changed the way the church views God, the body of Christ, and the world?

3. What kind of impact would you guess observing this church living out their faith in this way has had on their community, especially those who are not Christians?

4. From a missions standpoint, what are some ways you think this one act has changed the world?

5. Besides adoption, what are some other ways this group, along with others in your churches, could get involved in helping the orphan?

6. If you did even one or two of these things, how do you think it would change you, your church, your community, and the world for Christ?

HomeBuilders Principle:
Small steps of faithfulness to care for those close to God's heart will not only impact you and them, but also your church, your community, and the entire world.

A Spring of Water

7. Read Isaiah 58:10-12.

And if you give yourself to the hungry
And satisfy the desire of the afflicted,
Then your light will rise in darkness
And your gloom will become like midday.
And the LORD will continually guide you,
And satisfy your desire in scorched places,
And give strength to your bones;
And you will be like a watered garden,
And like a spring of water whose waters do
not fail.

According to this passage, what promises does God give to those who help the helpless? How would you apply these promises in your life?

Make a Date

Make a date with your spouse to meet before the next session to complete the HomeBuilders Project. Your leader will ask you to share something from this experience.

_____
DATE

_____
TIME

_____
LOCATION

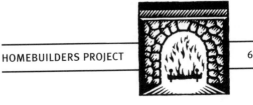
Now that you've spent a few weeks working through this decision as a couple, we suggest that you obtain some resources that will help you along in your journey. These are available through FamilyLife by calling 1-800-FL-TODAY (358-6329) or by visiting familylife.com.

"God's Heart for the Orphan," a message by Dennis Rainey (DVD).

Fields of the Fatherless, by C. Thomas Davis.

His Heart, Our Hands: A Guide for Establishing and Growing an Orphans Ministry in the local church, a booklet from FamilyLife's Hope for Orphans ministry.

Knowing
God Personally

Introduction

- For those who seek it, God provides the power necessary to fulfill His purposes and to carry out His plan for oneness.

- We cannot experience this power unless we know God personally. The following principles explain how to have a relationship with God.

1. God loves you and created you for a relationship with Him.

1. God loves you.

"For God so loved the world, that He gave His only begotten Son, that whoever believes in Him shall not perish, but have eternal life."

John 3:16

2. God wants you to know Him.

"And this is eternal life, that they may know You, the only true God, and Jesus Christ whom You have sent."

John 17:3

2. Humanity is separated from God and cannot know Him personally or experience His love and power.

a. All of us are sinful.

For all have sinned and fall short of the glory of God.

Romans 3:23

b. Our sin separates us from God.

For the wages of sin is death ...

Romans 6:23a

How can the gulf between God and man be bridged?

3. Jesus Christ is God's only provision for our sin. Through Him alone we can know God personally and experience His love.

a. God became a man in the Person of Jesus Christ.

The Word [Jesus] became flesh, and dwelt among us, and we saw His glory, glory as of the only begotten from the Father, full of grace and truth.

John 1:14

b. He died in our place.

But God demonstrates His own love toward us, in that while we were yet sinners, Christ died for us.

Romans 5:8

c. He rose from the dead.

Christ died for our sins ... He was buried ... He was raised on the third day according to the Scriptures ... He appeared to Cephas (Peter), then to the twelve. After that He appeared to more than five hundred ...

1 Corinthians 15:3-6

d. He is the only way to God.

Jesus said to him, "I am the way, and the truth, and the life; no one comes to the Father, but through Me."

John 14:6

4. We must individually receive Jesus Christ as Savior and Lord; then we can know God personally and experience His love.

a. We must change our minds about the way we have lived.

b. We must receive Christ by accepting the free gift of salvation He offers us.

But as many as received Him, to them He gave the right to become children of God, even to those who believe in His name.

John 1:12

For by grace you have been saved through faith; and that not of yourselves, it is the gift of God; not as a result of works, so that no one may boast.

Ephesians 2:8-9

Self-Directed Life   Christ-Directed Life

5. What are the results of placing my faith in Jesus Christ? The Bible says:

a. My sins are forgiven. (Colossians 2:13).

b. I possess the gift of eternal life.
And the testimony is this, that God has given us eternal life, and this life is in His Son.

1 John 5:11

c. I have been given the Holy Spirit to empower me to pursue intimacy with God and oneness with my spouse.

6. I can respond to God right now by faith through prayer.

A suggested life-changing decision: "Lord Jesus, I need You. Thank You for dying on the cross for my sins. I acknowledge that I am a sinner and I am separated from You. Please forgive me. I receive You as my Savior and Lord. Thank You for forgiving my sins and giving me eternal life. Please take control of my life. Make me the kind of person You want me to be."

Signature _____

Date _____

Leader's Tips

Leader qualifications

Leading a HomeBuilders group does not require an expert Bible teacher or even a couple with a "perfect" marriage. And leading this study on adoption does not require that you have a broad knowledge base about adoption. The leader of the group is a facilitator, not a lecturer. The main function of the facilitator is to provide an environment of openness, warmth, and acceptance.

The facilitator is a fellow member of the group who has the added responsibility of guiding the group in the right direction within the limited time period. The best leaders are couples willing to share their successes and weaknesses while trying to have a better marriage at the same time.

If you are unsure about your ability to lead, consider co-leading with another couple. You can divide the responsibilities. Trust God together to work in your lives and to help other couples.

Starting a HomeBuilders group

As a couple, commit to each other and to God to make the HomeBuilders group a priority for the time it will take to complete the study. (Remember, it only requires a short-term commitment. You may choose to meet weekly or every other week.) Decide how you will share responsibility for organizing and leading the group, preparing for the sessions, making phone calls, and extending hospitality.

Inviting couples to participate

If you have attended an "If You Were Mine" Adoption Workshop, consider asking other couples who attended to join your group. You may also want to ask your pastor if he knows of any couples who would be interested and if you could promote the group within the church (see below). There are often a small handful of couples in every church who have an interest in learning more about adoption.

Consider asking other area pastors about including a bulletin or "up front" announcement in their worship service. You may also want to call local adoption agencies and ask if there are couples that have contacted them that are involved in making decisions about adoption and might be interested in such a group. Invite friends, neighbors, co-workers, and parents from your children's school or sports. A personal invitation is always best.

If your church has an adoption/orphans ministry, this study could be implemented on a periodic basis (possibly once or twice a year) with an entirely new group of interested couples participating each time. This provides an ongoing opportunity for couples in your church to explore adoption when they are ready to do so.

Show potential group members the study materials and tell them about the discussion format. You will want to assure couples that they will be making a limited time commitment and that getting involved is by no means a commitment to pursue adoption. This study is designed to help people decide if they should pursue adoption.

An ideal size for the group is four-to-seven couples (including you and your spouse).

Child care

It is important that your group focus on the study material without distractions and interruptions. Ask your group what works best for them. Dependable child care is critical. Some couples will not be able to commit to every group session if childcare is not provided. Here are some suggestions:

- Arrange babysitting in one house and conduct the study in another.
- Pool financial resources to hire a babysitter.
- Ask if any couples have older children who would agree to baby-sit.
- Use available child care or church facilities.
- Hold your group meetings at the same time as Chapel Awana or other children's programs.

Leading a HomeBuilders group

Before you begin each session, agree as a couple how much to communicate about your own marriage, adoption, and adopted children (if applicable). Open sharing will help others apply biblical truths to their own lives. Study the Leader's Notes and pray regularly for your group. Also, discuss as a couple your leadership responsibilities for each session.

It is important to practice hospitality. Making friends is a key to creating an environment in which God will change lives. In our impersonal world, many couples are hungry for friendships. God will use your relationships in an atmosphere of mild accountability to encourage couples to apply the lessons to their lives. You may find that the members of your group will eventually make up the core of a Christian adoption support group in your church or community.

Starting the session

Share the following ground rules at the beginning of the first session, and review as needed:

- Share nothing that will embarrass your spouse.
- Pass on any question.
- Maintain confidentiality.
- Complete the HomeBuilders Project with spouses between sessions.

Simply read through the questions to lead the study. At first, you may need to wait for answers. Don't jump in too quickly with your own ideas; couples will wait for you and you will end up teaching the material without input from them. Ideas you can solicit from the group will mean more to the participants than those you "teach." When discussion is going too long or gets off the subject, just read the next question to stay on track.

Components of each session

Warm Up (15 minutes)

The purpose of Warm Up is to help people unwind from a busy day and get to know each other better. The questions also lead them toward the topic of that session.

Blueprints (60 minutes)

This is the heart of the study. In this category, people answer pertinent questions related to the topic of study and look to God's Word for understanding.

Wrap Up (15 minutes)

This section serves to "bring home the point" and wind down a session in an appropriate fashion.

HomeBuilders Project (60 minutes)

This is the unique application step in a HomeBuilders study. Before your meeting ends, couples are encouraged to "Make a

Date" to complete this project with their spouse before the next meeting. Encourage couples to make this a priority—it will make the HomeBuilders experience twice as effective.

Additional tips

1. Keep the focus on what Scripture says. When someone disagrees with Scripture, affirm him for wrestling with the issue and point out that some biblical statements are hard to understand or accept. Encourage him to keep an open mind on the issue through the remainder of the sessions.

2. Avoid labeling an answer as "wrong"—doing so can kill the atmosphere for discussion. Encourage a person who gives a wrong or incomplete answer to look again at the question or the Scripture being explored. Offer a comment such as, "That's really close" or "There's something else we need to see there." Or ask others in the group to respond.

3. Your best resource for communicating with others is your own life and marriage. Be prepared to get the discussion going by sharing things from your own lives. But as a couple, be sure that you agree beforehand about the issues and experiences.

Praying in the group

An important part of a small group is prayer. Be sensitive to the comfort level of group members about praying in front of others. Never call on people to pray aloud if you don't know if they are comfortable doing this. There are a number of creative approaches you can take; such as modeling prayer, calling for volunteers, and letting people pray in the form of finishing a sentence. A helpful tool is to create a prayer list. Lead the prayer time, but allow another couple the opportunity to create, update, and distribute prayer lists as a group ministry.

Refreshments

Many groups choose to have refreshments to create an environment of fellowship. Some suggestions include:

- For the first session or two offer refreshments and then allow the group to be involved by providing a sign-up sheet.
- Consider starting your group with a short time of informal fellowship and refreshment (15 minutes), then move into the study. If a couple arrives late, the study is not disrupted.

Building new leadership

Look for potential leaders who might multiply your group into new groups. Someone may even express interest in leading. Here are a few pointers to help build new leaders:

- Look for those who demonstrate availability, teachability, and faithfulness.
- Select a couple who demonstrates maturity in their Christian walk and marriage, and whom you feel would be good discussion leaders. Challenge them to lead.
- Invite the couple to try the leadership role by asking one or two questions, leading part of the session, and then leading an entire session by the end of the study.
- Issue the challenge to start a group after the current study is completed.

Leader's Notes

Here are some additional notes about various Blueprints questions and possible answers, if you should need further assistance. The numbers below correspond to the Blueprints question numbers. Notes are not included for every question. Most questions are designed to assure that group members understand scriptural principles.

Many study questions are also designed so group members can draw from their own opinions and experiences. If you share any of these points, be sure to do so in a manner that does not stifle discussion by making you the authority with the final answers. Begin your comments by saying things like, "One thing I notice in this passage is ... " or "I think another reason for this is ...."

Session One

Question #8: Bringing any child, adopted or biological, into a home can result in various types of difficulties. If this couple never resolves this unity issue, the difficulties that will inevitably arise with their adopted child will cause great marital strain. The draggee may become resentful toward the dragger for "getting them into this to begin with." In addition, the dragger will grow frustrated that the draggee remains disengaged through the parenting process.

Question #9: Caring for the fatherless is a very high priority to God. Out of all things He could have used to define "pure and lasting religion" (Bible study, tithing, prayer, church attendance, etc.), He listed caring for two groups of people who often don't have a voice in society.

Question #10: One possible answer to this question is that orphans generally can't repay you. Caring for them is very often a completely selfless act.

Question #11 Adoption is a transaction that God has not only sanctioned but has demonstrated for us. Adoption as an act of redemption is woven into the very story of God's love for us.

Session Two

Question #1: At the time that these texts were recorded, these three groups of people were in an especially precarious position. Not only was their ability to produce income minimal, but they also had a very limited capacity to maintain their rights in that society. They were often taken advantage of by others who were more powerful.

Question #6: Some examples would be: fight, protect, argue, act, guard, push, prevent, block, respond, etc,

Question #8: Adoption is a legal transaction by which a child gains all the rights and responsibilities of a biological child. An adopted child experiences the same benefits as a birth child. When we were adopted in Christ; all the rights, responsibilities, and benefits of being a member of God's family were given to us. In God's eyes our standing is no different than if we were naturally born into His family.

Session Three

Question #6: It is extremely common for couples pursuing adoption to feel overwhelmed for a variety of reasons. For some, these feelings are related to infertility. For others it is financial concerns or family objections. Regardless of the concerns, these passages illustrate God's provision for his children in their time of concern and worry.

Question #7: One of the keys of this passage as it relates to adoption is that God had already spent years preparing Moses for what He had called him to do. The problem was not that Moses wasn't equipped. The problem was that Moses didn't *feel* equipped. Often we are equipped for things we don't *feel* equipped for.

Question #8: Angela's parents' bring up a variety of issues, but it seems that all of them have a common source: They are concerned about their children and grandchildren's well-being. Ultimately their motivation is love and concern, though they do not handle their feelings in the most constructive manner.

Session Four

Question #4: Some answers might include: Adoption agency background information, agency experience and referrals, agency fee structures, adoption process information, country specific information for international adoption, funding assistance alternatives, and information on bringing an adopted child into your current family context. These possibilities are just a few of the many pieces of information a couple may need in order to make an informed adoption decision.

Question #9: God uses His Holy Spirit to guide us as we seek to make wise decisions.

Question #10: Often adoption is seen as a matter of personal preference when in fact it is one of the many possible obedient responses to God's repeated command to look after the orphan.

Question #11: This understanding changes the paradigm of the adoption decision from, "I want to get a child for my family that will satisfy my desires" to, "I want to give a child a family as an obedient response to God's desires."

Session Five

Question #5: FamilyLife's booklet *His Heart, Our Hands: A Guide to Establishing and Growing Orphans Ministry in the Local Church* provides practical answers to this question.